Original title:
Sands of the Soul

Copyright © 2025 Creative Arts Management OÜ
All rights reserved.

Author: Julian Carmichael
ISBN HARDBACK: 978-1-80581-677-5
ISBN PAPERBACK: 978-1-80581-204-3
ISBN EBOOK: 978-1-80581-677-5

Portraits of the Quiet

In shadows where whispers play,
A cat naps, dreaming away.
The toaster skips breakfast songs,
While the clock ticks, righting the wrongs.

In corners where dust bunnies lie,
A lost sock starts a shy sigh.
The bookshelves hold secrets untold,
Where quiet matters are bold and old.

A chair creaks with a chuckle low,
As if it knows all we don't show.
The fridge hums a tune so sly,
While leftover pizza aims to fly.

In each echo, a humor sweet,
A home where the ordinary meets.
Behind the silence, a wink and a grin,
The stillness is louder than anything.

Ethereal Landscapes of Longing

In the desert of dreams, I lost my shoe,
My laces are tangled like a bad déjà vu.
The mirage laughs, waving a flag,
While I dance with a cactus, oh what a brag!

Beneath the stars, my map's a joke,
Finding the path, I'll need a folk.
The breeze tickles as I trip on a rock,
I swear the moon just winked, mock and mock.

Threads Woven in the Silence.

I knitted my dreams with yarn that was blue,
But ended up stitching my cat to my shoe.
The silence is loud, it giggles and teases,
As I talk to the plants, which I think are geniuses.

In the quiet of night, I sip on some tea,
But it spills on my lap, oh laugh with me!
The threads of my thoughts are tangled and bright,
I toast to the moon for a wild, silly night.

Whispers of Time

Tick-tock whispers, time's got a jest,
It pulls at my sleeve while I try to rest.
I blinked too fast, now it's Tuesday twice,
My calendar insists it thinks it's so nice.

I chase after moments like a dog with a cat,
But they slip through my fingers, like a game of pat.
The seconds giggle, they snicker and run,
I'll catch them next time, oh, won't that be fun?

Echoes Across the Dunes

Across the hills, my laughter rolls,
While I lose my grip on my pancake goals.
The echoes bounce back, saying, 'Oops, not so fast,'
I'm sliding on sand in a race with the past.

With every tumble, I giggle with glee,
The dunes keep on laughing, all mirthful and free.
In this whimsical world of sandy delight,
I'll find my lost marbles, they're just out of sight.

Dreams in the Dunes

In a desert of socks, my dreams took flight,
Chasing tumbleweeds on a hot summer night.
I danced with a cactus, we twirled and spun,
Laughed out loud as the setting sun.

A mirage of ice cream, I raced in delight,
But all I found was a lizard in sight.
We shared a sweet laugh, then parted ways,
He wore a top hat, oh what a gaze!

Buried treasure appeared with a wink,
Just an old shoe—now that's some stink!
Yet still, dreams linger, as wild winds blow,
In the laughter of dunes, where silliness flows.

The Quest for Identity

Who am I, a sock or a shoe?
A mixed-up puzzle - what must I do?
I tried on a hat that was far too tight,
Then stumbled and fell, oh what a sight!

Climbed up a mountain of mismatched pairs,
Yelled to the heavens, 'Who cares? Who dares?'
A squirrel in a cape shouted back, 'It's grand!'
'Just wear what you love, let your heart be your brand!'

With each outfit change, I lost my way,
Now I'm a rainbow, come join the display!
In a quest of a lifetime, here's my decree,
Be ridiculous, be you, and set your soul free!

Beyond the Horizon

The horizon was wobbly, a jelly-like sight,
I leaped with a friend, ready for flight.
We packed our snacks: chips, and jelly beans,
For adventures unseen, like wizards and queens!

Climbing the clouds, we stumbled in laughter,
Hitching a ride with a kite up the rafters.
A seagull wearing glasses squawked out a tune,
Making us giggle beneath the bright moon.

The world was a circus, a twist and a spin,
Life's like confetti, let the fun begin!
So fly beyond limits, choose silly over wise,
For joy is the treasure that never denies.

The Faces of Solitude

Oh solitude, you jokester, you sly little tease,
Knocked on my door, brought snacks and some cheese.
With a grin on your face, like a cat in the sun,
You told me alone is just learning to run.

I met my reflection, it made a funny face,
Poked at my cheeks, we shared a small space.
We took silly selfies of two lonely souls,
Drawing mustaches and silly remarks on the scrolls.

You showed me the joy in a day spent inside,
Hoarding my thoughts like treasures to hide.
So here's to the laughter solitude brings,
In the silence, I find my heart sings!

Shifting Landscapes Within

In the mind's vast barren land,
Thoughts twist and tumble, unplanned.
A tumbleweed rolls by with flair,
Waving hats, in a wispy air.

Mountains of laundry, they grow high,
Where lost socks and dreams play shy.
I searched for wisdom, found a snack,
Now the wisdom's on my track!

A mirage of wisdom, bright and clear,
Turns to jellybeans, oh dear!
Navigating life with glee and cheer,
But always tripping on my beer.

So, here's to the wild ride inside,
With giggles, wiggles, and a side slide.
To worry less about the fray,
And laugh at the chaos every day.

Dust Storm of Dreams

In a whirlwind, dreams take flight,
Like socks that vanish in the night.
Dusty visions whirl and twirl,
Tickling noses, a sneezy swirl.

I dream of cookies, freshly baked,
But wake to find the snacks have flaked.
A chocolate-chip mirage I see,
Dancing in front of me, oh me!

With each puff of gusty chatter,
Plans dissolve, but dreams still splatter.
I paint my future bright and loud,
While spilling juice, oh, I'm so proud!

So let the storm spin dreams around,
In a playful whirly gigging sound.
Reality's just a cheesy jest,
With laughter being the very best.

Beneath the Surface

Underneath my surface, what a scene,
A circus of chaos, it's quite routine.
Thoughts like clowns, all dressed in bright,
Juggling worries, in black and white.

Beneath that grin, a noodle bends,
Spaghetti thoughts, they don't make amends.
Twists and turns in my noodle mind,
Oh, the treasures I've left behind!

With a pop and fizz, new ideas rise,
Like balloons escaping to the skies.
I chase them down with a goofy glee,
But end up stuck in my own debris!

So here's to the fun below the skin,
With all the dreams that dance and spin.
Life's a jest beneath the frown,
A hidden comedy in this town.

Traces of the Unseen

In the silence, giggles hide,
With whispers of things that can't abide.
A chair that creaks with every move,
Is it a ghost or dance to groove?

Dust bunnies form a troupe so sly,
Plotting mischief as they fly.
With tiny hats and shoes to match,
Racing snails, the perfect catch!

In shadows lurk the playful spry,
With pixie laughter floating by.
Chasing dreams that feel so close,
But always just a playful dose!

So cheers to the unseen, oh so bright,
Filling our days with pure delight.
For in the quiet, we'll find the scene,
Of giggles and gigas, so unseen!

Dreams Etched in Time

Dreams tumble like socks in a dryer,
Spinning tales while we both conspire.
A fleeting thought in morning's gleam,
Chasing giggles in a waking dream.

We danced like noodles in boiling pots,
Wearing hats made of paper and knots.
Time tickles us with a jolly laugh,
Counting moments in a bouncy raft.

Frogs in tuxedos leap through the air,
Waving party hats without a care.
A clock sings loudly, tickling rhymes,
While we juggle our half-sweet limes.

Every tick brings a waltzy tune,
As we waltz past the silver moon.
Smiles and chuckles in a time parade,
Dancing in shadows, lightly displayed.

The Language of Light

Light winks at us with a cheeky grin,
Shadows chuckle as the day begins.
A glowstick tells secrets in the dark,
While fireflies gather for a spark.

In the twilight, we wear silly hats,
Shooting stars zoom past like acrobats.
A disco ball spins in the summer breeze,
While moonbeams shimmy through the trees.

Laughter bounces like a rubber ball,
Tickling the edges of night's soft shawl.
We speak in giggles, a burst of cheer,
Light-hearted whispers to chase away fear.

Every flicker is a story told,
With hues of warmth in shades of gold.
As lumens dance in their frolicking flight,
We write our tales in the language of light.

Resilience of Shadows

Shadows stretch like silly putty seams,
Bending and twisting, revealing dreams.
In the corner, a shadow jives,
Dancing to tunes of our crazy lives.

They hide and seek with every glance,
Wearing capes, they join our dance.
Poking fun at our flailing prance,
Invisible partners in a wild romance.

A shadow yawns and takes a nap,
While sunlight plays a cheeky slap.
We giggle at the shapes that yield,
As our laughter echoes on the field.

In every dark, there's a light to find,
Witty reflections of the curious kind.
Shadows giggle, with a bounce and a sway,
Carving their tales in the light of day.

Where Time Stands Still

In a pocket watch filled with jelly beans,
Time slows down, or so it seems.
We sit on clouds, having a feast,
Waiting for seconds; oh, what a tease!

Ticktock goes the chocolate clock,
As we stroll on wobbly rock.
Moments pass like a balloon on a string,
Each pop brings laughter, a silly fling.

Cucumbers wear hats while onions waltz,
Zucchini joins in, without a pause.
With each tick, we share a pie,
Chasing whispers where time is shy.

So let us frolic in this surreal space,
Where laughter rings and moments race.
Caught forever in this brilliant thrill,
In a world where time stands absolutely still.

Footprints in the Ether

I tripped on dreams while walking light,
They vanished quick, oh what a sight.
My slippers danced, but I did not,
Chasing echoes that I forgot.

With each step, I lost a shoe,
The clouds just giggled, how rude, it's true.
I leaped for stars, but slipped on air,
Now they're stuck in my messy hair.

Laughter floats on winds that tease,
Tickling noses with gentle breeze.
My footprints left in fields of thought,
Where giggles linger and truth is sought.

Now count the steps, a mile away,
Who knew thoughts could so easily sway?
In this waltz, my heart just skips,
While I chase giggles and stardust trips.

Sculpting Tomorrow

With clay in hand, my future's bright,
I molded dreams on misty nights.
But my ambitions rolled away,
Like dogs that chase a bright bouquet.

I sculpted hopes, a funny beast,
With three left feet and a turkey feast.
When trying for the great and grand,
A potato formed instead of sand.

Life's a canvas cheekily bare,
I painted smiles with time to spare.
In every brush a silly twist,
Tomorrow's art, you get the gist.

Now laughter's all that I can craft,
With each mistake, I find the laugh.
Tomorrow's secrets, oops and all,
Are just my sculptures upon the wall.

Among the Whispers

Among the whispers in the breeze,
I heard a joke that brought me to my knees.
The trees were gossiping, oh so sly,
About the squirrel who thought he could fly.

The wind chimed in with a giggling tune,
As clouds chuckled under a laughing moon.
Each rustle shared a silly truth,
Like how the fountain lost a tooth.

In this realm of chortles and cheer,
I found the truest friends right here.
The bushes winked, the flowers danced,
Each giggle held a silly chance.

So join the revelry and play the fool,
In this paradise, I found my school.
Among the whispers, life unfolds,
With jest and laughter that never grows old.

A Tapestry of Transience

I wove a tale of threads so bright,
But yarn unraveled in mid-flight.
Each stitch a joke, each knot a grin,
Now it's a blanket I can't fit in.

With colors wild and patterns strange,
I crafted moments that love would change.
Yet my masterpiece turned into fluff,
Looks like life thought that was enough.

From threads of laughs, the fabric flows,
In every loop, a giggle grows.
I stitched my heart to every seam,
But the needle slipped, oh, what a dream!

So here I sit with fabric strange,
In this tapestry, I must arrange.
For life is short, and laughter long,
A woven wonder, where I belong.

The Pulse of the Winds

A breeze tickles at my nose,
Whispers of laughter, goodness knows.
The trees bend low, share a joke,
While a squirrel steals an acorn cloak.

In twirls of gusts, they leap and spin,
Dance like the fools we find within.
With every gust, a giggle flies,
As even clouds break into sighs.

The wind rushes, tickles my hair,
Playing tag with the ghost of air.
A kite goes soaring, what a sight,
Was that a bird or a shirt in flight?

With breezy puns, the world spins round,
As tumbleweeds make funny sounds.
Life's a circus, spinning around,
In every breeze, a jest is found.

In the Wake of Echoes

In valleys deep, laughter rings,
Echoes bounce with little wings.
Shouts of joy from hills nearby,
Where even rocks burst into sighs.

Please don't ask where whispers flee,
They giggle off, just let them be.
In every hollow, jokes abound,
As old stones crack with silly sound.

In twilight's glow, they play their game,
Chasing giggles, never lame.
A voice says, "Hello? Who's there?"
Only a mouse with fuzzy hair!

Each echo's tale, a jest divine,
Bounces back with a funny line.
In the theater of the night,
Every noise brings pure delight.

Waters of the Ancient Past

In bubbling brooks, the fish do grin,
Splashing water, cheeky kin.
With every jump, they tease and weave,
"Catch me if you can!" they cleave.

Old rivers chuckle as they wind,
Tales of mischief left behind.
Currents dance with a playful swish,
Water sprites tell jokes in a fish dish.

Oh, the tales the ripples impart,
Silly stories, a classic art.
Paddles splash with glee and jest,
As every wave is nature's fest.

With every drop, the laughter flows,
As lily pads wear froggy clothes.
The water's winks and playful splashes,
Bring giggles on with each wave's crashes.

The Dance of the Invisible

Invisible friends, oh what fun,
They spin and twirl, a crazy run.
In empty halls, they laugh and play,
Turning shadows into a ballet.

Tickle the air with a gentle touch,
They hang around, they love to clutch.
With every flicker of candlelight,
They steal the scene and take flight.

In the quiet, they whisper loud,
Making mischief, oh so proud.
A ghostly giggle floats through space,
As they dash for an unseen race.

So here's to the dance we cannot see,
The silly twirl of mystery.
In laughter's echo, they reside,
A lively crew, our playful guide.

The Desert of Desire

In a land where cacti play hide and seek,
A mirage of cookies, oh so antique.
The tumbleweeds dance, they've got some flair,
Chasing dreams of a picnic without a care.

With every sip from an empty flask,
It's the thirst for laughter, that's our task.
A lizard in shades, strutting with pride,
Who knew the dunes could be such a ride?

Here in the heat, we'll create our cheer,
Building sandcastles of snacks and beer.
The sun can be harsh, we wear it well,
In this comedy, we'll laugh and dwell.

So come join the fun, let's not be shy,
We'll roast marshmallows under the sky.
With laughter that echoes, we'll rule this place,
In the desert of wishes, we'll leave our trace.

Remnants of Radiance

In the glow of late night campfires bright,
We share silly stories, oh what delight!
Ghosts in the shadows, they tell us to hush,
But we're too busy laughing, we'll always rush.

Glowworms above get jealous we shine,
As we fumble with guitars and sing off the line.
With marshmallow mustaches, we fight for the last,
Who knew such a treat could go by so fast?

Reflections of joy dance in the night,
As we juggle mischief under the light.
Stars giggle above at the chaos we've made,
In remnants of fun, our laughter won't fade.

So here's to our shenanigans, let's raise a cheer,
In this quirky realm, there's nothing to fear.
With memories sparkling, like stars far and wide,
We'll carry this magic right by our side.

Timeless Revelations

In the hourglass of giggles, time slips away,
With wisecracks and puns that come out to play.
We find in the chaos a comic delight,
Awakening laughter that tickles the night.

With each grain that falls, a jest is revealed,
Secrets of silliness, hilariously concealed.
Surprises tumble out like confetti on cue,
Each moment a treasure, forever brand new.

The echoes of chuckles blend with the breeze,
While shadows wobble under the trees.
Who would've thought that time could be fun?
In timeless revelations, our hearts weigh a ton.

So let's gather our quirks and let them unroll,
Delighted in folly, we dance with our soul.
In this realm of mischief, let's take our stance,
For laughter's our treasure; we'll always prance.

Silhouette Beneath the Stars

Under a blanket of twinkling lights,
We find hidden gems and curious sights.
Silhouettes dancing, what a delight,
With shadows that swerve in hilarious flight.

A raccoon wearing glasses steals our snacks,
While fireflies laugh at our silly hijacks.
With goofy poses, we strike our best shot,
Captured in laughter, we forget what we've got.

The moon's a comedian, glowing so bright,
Tossing us punchlines while we hold on tight.
A play in the garden, with critters our cast,
In this whimsical theater, forever will last.

Beneath all the stars, we each play our role,
Crafting our moments, it's good for the soul.
So let's dance in the dark, let the night unfurl,
In the silhouette stories, we're kings of the swirl.

The Weight of a Breath

A heavy sigh, a thought so light,
Like lifting feathers in flight.
Each breath I take, a quirky dance,
Inhale, exhale, my kind of prance.

A tickle here, a wheeze up there,
My lungs are not in peak repair.
But still I puff and blow with glee,
Who knew breathing could be so free?

With every chuckle, there's a wheeze,
A symphony from lungs with ease.
Carbon dioxide's my spirit mate,
Together we laugh, we celebrate.

So take a breath, embrace the fun,
Inhaling life, till day is done.
Exhaling joy, like balloons in flight,
Who knew breath could feel so light?

Eternal Shifts

The clock ticks on with cheeky grins,
Moments waltz, but time just spins.
Like socks that vanish in the wash,
Shifts happen fast, oh what a posh!

Yesterday's snacks are tomorrow's tales,
A twist of fate like bouncing whales.
While we chase clocks and scrolls and tweets,
Eternal shifts just bring us treats.

Moods flip like pancakes on a griddle,
Sometimes you're serious, then a riddle.
Like seasons that dance and play their tunes,
Life's a party with unknown boons.

So laugh and twirl through change with grace,
Finding humor in every face.
Embrace the chaos, take a chance,
For every shift is a funny dance!

Harmony in Emptiness

In the quiet where echoes play,
I trip on silence, what a ballet!
Each empty room has a laugh to share,
   Whispers chuckle in vacant air.

A chasm of space, a chorus loud,
Where nothing thunders, proud and bowed.
Yet in this void, I found my muse,
A costumed ghost with silly shoes.

The gaps between, they giggle too,
In every pause, a joke rings true.
Emptiness hums its funny tune,
My heart beats wild like an empty room.

So dance with nothing, feel the cheer,
For absence sings when we are near.
Lighten the load, feel the jest,
In the harmony where voids are blessed.

Deserted Reveries

In dreams that drift like tumbleweeds,
I wander through imaginary fields.
Chasing thoughts like lizards fast,
One moment here, the next—oh blast!

No one's around, just me and stars,
In a crowd of dreams, nobody spars.
My mind plays tricks, like a magic show,
With invisible friends that laugh and throw.

Each corner turned, a hat—surprise!
I trip on jokes that never die.
In this deserted land of dreams,
Reality's nothing but silly schemes.

So join me in this quirky spree,
Where thought and laughter run so free.
In deserted realms, come take a stroll,
Exploring the humor that fills the soul.

Transient Paths of the Spirit

A wandering thought on a whim,
Chasing the light, feeling quite dim.
A tangle of giggles, a slip on a shoe,
Who knew enlightenment could be so askew?

The heart takes a detour, a laugh at the moon,
Where else can one find a lost tune?
Dancing in circles, a dizzying spree,
Life's little mishaps are all we can see.

With spirits unshackled, we stumble with grace,
Funny how wisdom can hide in the chase.
The spirit will wander, it won't take a toll,
Finding the fancy in every odd stroll.

Footprints in the Mind's Gallery

In the gallery's corners, strange shadows parade,
Unearthly memories in vibrant charade.
Who painted the picture that looks like my sock?
I swear these odd canvases keep me in shock.

An artist's hand slips; it just cannot blend,
Colors of chaos, say, is that my old friend?
With whimsical strokes, they create a pretzel,
Oh, what a masterpiece made from a vessel!

The brush tickles thoughts in a humorous way,
Never a dull moment in this playful fray.
As each footprint echoes a giggle or two,
The soul keeps on laughing, what else can it do?

Celestial Dust and Hidden Depths

Under the stars, a spark starts to fly,
What's that glimmering? Oh my, oh my!
It's just cosmic crumbs from that last space feast,\nFloating around like a quirky little beast.

The universe whispers a joke on repeat,
"I'm full of surprises; you'll laugh at my feet!"
As dust entertains with its magnificent twirl,
Hidden depths chuckle in an intergalactic whirl.

With comets that wink and galaxies grin,
Life's celestial circus has just now begun.
So giggle and frolic through the night sky's sweep,
For even the cosmos has secrets to keep!

Slow Reveal of the Inner Tapestry

A threadbare secret, unraveled with time,
Each twist and each turn, a joke in its rhyme.
What's hidden behind this silly facade?
Is it humor or wisdom or a little bit odd?

The loom creaks and laughs at our tangled designs,
Knots of confusion, oh where are the signs?
With each tug and pull, the colors do blend,
And life hands us punchlines with each little bend.

As layers unfold like a chronicle's jest,
The heart finds a chuckle and feels truly blessed.
So truth might be funny, as it wraps us in glee,
In the tapestry's pattern, let's dance carefree!

Treasures in the Dust

Once I found a sock in the dust,
Thought it held a fortune, a glorious bust.
But it sniffed, and it stunk, and it ran away,
Leaving me alone for another dull day.

Then there was a penny, all rusty and green,
Claimed it was magic, but it looked quite mean.
I tried to flip it, but didn't quite know,
So it rolled to the cat and then said, "Hello!"

Buried in dirt, a toy from my youth,
A plastic dinosaur with a toothy truth.
It's quite a thrill when you dig and you find,
That life's just a joke, and we're all quite blind.

So here in my corner, I crouch and I weave,
Dissecting the detritus, learning to grieve.
For every lost treasure, a chuckle, a scoff,
The laughter of relics, we're better off!

Touching the Ethereal

Once I tried to dance with a ghost so spry,
Thought he'd teach me moves that would make me fly.
But he tripped on a table and fell through the floor,
Now I'm left here laughing, it's never a bore.

I reached for a cloud, thought I'd take it for tea,
It slipped right away, said, "You cannot kid me!"
With a puff and a giggle, it rained on my hat,
Now I'm soaked and confused by my fluffy friend, that.

Chasing wisps of thoughts that dance on the breeze,
I caught one and shouted, "Oh, do as you please!"
It whispered back softly, then tied up my tongue,
Now I speak in riddles, can't say I was hung.

On nights when the stars wink, I ponder and muse,
The fluff and the fluffier, it's quite a ruse.
For nothing is serious, it's all in the jest—
Life's an absurd stage, and I'm just a guest!

A Poem of Particles

In the realm of the tiny, they bounce and they sway,
Atoms are parting, like kids out to play.
One bumped into me, said, "Hey, what's the rush?"
I laughed at the chaos—the universe's crush.

Electrons are giggling, they spin and they twirl,
Protons are blushing in a subatomic whirl.
Neutrons just shrug, like, "What's the big deal?"
As I try to catch one, it gives me a squeal!

The particles prance, they're a jolly old crew,
They push and they pull, and they look right at you.
Amongst all their frolic, I ponder my fate,
Am I but a joke in this quantum estate?

So next time you think of the cosmic ballet,
Remember it's funny, it's never cliché.
For in each tiny moment, there's humor galore,
Just laugh with the particles, and you'll want more!

The Voice of the Void

In the silence of emptiness, echoes do play,
With whispers of nothingness that take me away.
I yelled into nothing, it shouted right back,
Said, "Your jokes are so bad, they should stay in the black!"

The void's quite the critic, with zero remorse,
It chuckles and mocks, like it's got no force.
"Hey, is this all?" it snickers with glee,
"You can't win at laughing, you're still out to sea!"

So I wrote a great story about all my loss,
The void turned to me and promptly laughed, "You're a doss!"
I took that as praise; I'm a star in my show,
Even if the audience is just me and the flow.

From the depths of existence, we riff and we rhyme,
In this grand cosmic joke, we're just wasting time.
So here's to the emptiness, full of delight,
For every good laugh, we'll dance through the night!

The Canvas of Solstice

On a canvas bright, I paint my fears,
With a brush made of jelly, amid chuckled cheers.
A sunset that giggles, under a silly sun,
Where shadows dance wildly, just for fun.

The colors collide, like creatures of flight,
A polka-dotted sky welcomes the night.
With crayons in hand, I scribble my dreams,
While sipping on lemonade with marshmallow streams.

Dancing with rabbits, painting the leaves,
As pineapples whistle and dandelions tease.
A landscape of laughter, my canvas unfolds,
In the solstice of giggles, my story is told.

The Silken Thread of Memory

A thread made of giggles, so soft and so fine,
Weaving experience, like sipping on wine.
With each twist and turn, memories hum,
Like a cat chasing yarn or a spicy hot bun.

In a tapestry bright, I stitch all the woes,
With glimmers of laughter where sunshine flows.
Each loop holds a secret, a joke or a pun,
As the fabric of life invites everyone.

In corners of humor, my threads intertwine,
Reminiscing the times when jellies would shine.
I chuckle at moments that made me a fool,
With threads of delight, I color my pool.

The Color of Winds

Whispers of blues and a dash of bright green,
With a swirl of giggles that none have seen.
The breezes are chuckling, swirling around,
As the trees shake their branches, up off the ground.

Howling in laughter, the winds tell their tales,
With echoes of jokers riding furious gales.
They tickle the daisies, and spin through the air,
Bringing surprises, and joy everywhere.

Clouds puff like marshmallows in the wide sky,
As breezes bring whispers of "Oh, my, oh my!"
A flavor of whimsy, a scent so wild,
In the color of winds, my inner child smiled.

Beneath the Veil

Behind a curtain of giggles and sighs,
A world of wonder, underneath it lies.
Where chuckles unfold, like magic on cue,
And laughter's a currency, traded by few.

A jester's hat peeks, creating delight,
As the moon shares secrets with stars shining bright.
With a wink to the shadows, to dreams so absurd,
In the embrace of humor, life's voice is heard.

Beneath the veil, in a dreamlike jest,
We frolic and tumble, and never let rest.
With hearts made of wonder, and socks mismatched,
In the land of the silly, we'll never detach.

Whispers of the Grain

In the desert's grand parade,
Little grains start to invade.
Each one wants a tale to tell,
Of bartering with the wishing well.

A grain once dreamed of being gold,
But got lost in a sunburned fold.
Now it hides beneath a stone,
Claiming turf, but feels alone.

With a giggle, the grains conspire,
Plotting schemes to rise and tire.
A grain with a swagger walks the line,
Faking riches, it's a real fine dine.

So let them dance upon the breeze,
With hopes of riches or a tease.
These grains of joy, bright and free,
Whisper secrets, just for me.

The Shifting Dunes of Being

In life's vast stretch, we often sway,
Like dunes that change with the light of day.
One moment wise like a sage,
Next, a tumbleweed on a stage.

A philosopher grain thinks it knows best,
While others roll by, playing jest.
"Why chase the sun?" one bemoans,
"Let's just nap and roll on stones!"

With a giggle, they'll flip and whirl,
Each grain a dancer, giving it a twirl.
But oh, the trouble, when one gets stuck,
It's a grain of sorrow, out of luck.

So laugh with the grains, embrace the tease,
Life's silly moments, like a breeze.
We blend, we shift, we dance, we sing,
In this grainy life, we're all a thing.

Echoes Beneath the Footsteps

Each step we take, a whisper's heard,
Underfoot's laughter, life's absurd.
Crumbly echoes giggle and tease,
"Hey, watch your step! We're not at ease!"

"Careful now, don't walk too fast!"
"Remember, buddy, grains can be a blast!"
Each footprint a letter of our youth,
Imprints of laughter, shadows of truth.

The grains exchange tales of the past,
Of slip-ups golden, memories cast.
Each misstep, a novel, wild and grand,
A comedy show upon the sand.

So step lightly, enjoy the ride,
Each grain beneath you has a side.
With echoes that giggle, boisterous and free,
In the land of laughter, come dance with me!

Timeless Particles

In a cosmos of woes, the particles play,
Full of mischief, come what may.
They slip and slide in a cosmic ball,
No time for seriousness, just a brawl!

A smidgen of this and a pinch of that,
Particles talking, imagine the chat!
"Let's create a new star!" one yells with glee,
"Or maybe just a black hole for tea!"

With tiny giggles, they swirl and twist,
Making futures that can't be missed.
Timeless jesters in cosmic embrace,
In the universe's laughter, we find our place.

With every dance, a joke or two,
Particles giggle, creating anew.
So let's toast to these moments bright,
In this timeless realm, we find pure light.

Mirage of Existence

In the desert of thought, where ideas roam,
A cactus does a jig, finding its home.
Lizards wear shades, sunbathing with style,
While camels are plotting their next big smile.

Through the heatwave of life, we dance and we twirl,
Water's just a whim, a mirage in a whirl.
We search for the truth in a disco ball light,
But tomorrow's hangover will surely be bright.

Reality's a joke, with punchlines to share,
Like socks in the sand, no matching but fair.
While echoes of laughter bounce off distant rocks,
We tiptoe on laughter, in flip-flop socks.

So raise up your cup filled with desert-made dream,
Let's toast to the fun in a sunbeam's gleam.
For though we are lost in this whimsical race,
We'll find joy in the chaos, a wild embrace.

Driftwood of the Heart

A heart like driftwood, it floats on the sea,
With barnacles whispering, 'Life's easy, be free!'
It dodges the waves, does a shimmy and sway,
While seagulls throw jokes like a comedic bouquet.

Bobbing through tides, with a chuckle or two,
It meets a poor clam that just dreams of the blue.
'Why worry?' says driftwood, 'You're destined to shine!'
But the clam just responds, 'I prefer to recline.'

So they float on together, a hilarious crew,
With laughter as bubbling as morning's fresh dew.
In each little splash, there's a tale that they tell,
Of fish who wear bow ties and swim rather well.

And as they drift past, on this whimsical quest,
They find joy in nonsense, they never check guest.
For love's in the ride, not the place you set sail,
With driftwood and laughter, they'll always prevail.

Petals on a Forgotten Shore

Petals on beaches where seagulls take bets,
They gossip about seashells and sandy regrets.
With waves crashing softly, a rhythm divine,
Even crabs on the sand know it's party time.

A flower squints bright in a sun-soaked display,
It dances with breezes, come what may.
Contemplating life while getting tan lines,
Just shouting aloud all its cheeky designs.

The tide rolls in gossip of love-stuck sea stars,
Who dream of the day they'll drift into bars.
With cocktails in hand made from kelp and some foam,
They plot their adventures, each wave a new home.

So here on this shore, where silliness grows,
We pick up the petals, as laughter bestows.
And cherish the whimsy, though it come and it go,
For life is a giggle, just riding the flow.

The Essence of Erosion

Time's funny, I swear, like a jester in drag,
Chipping away at mountains, it's a comedy swag.
With each little raindrop, the rocks smile with glee,
While boulders just gossip, 'Who's next, you or me?'

Erosion's a prankster, relentless and sly,
It's sculpting new shapes, oh me, oh my!
The earth shakes with laughter, the valleys take note,
As pebbles roll down in their cozy wet coat.

We giggle at cliffs as they tumble and sway,
'You're all washed up,' they chuckle, 'make way for less clay!'
Through cracks and through crevices, silly things bloom,
Like daisies that grow in a rocky old room.

So let's celebrate change with a dance or a jig,
In this land of mishaps, life's lessons are big.
For every great tumble can lead to a throne,
Where laughter erodes all the feelings alone.

The Heart's Shifting Desert

In a land where cacti play,
A lizard sings the blues all day.
With every twist, my heart will dance,
In the dust of love's sweet chance.

The sun is hot, the laughter loud,
I trip and fall, and feel so proud.
A tumbleweed rolls by with flair,
It whispers secrets, I just stare.

In this quirky, sandy zone,
Each grain a tale, a humor grown.
My heart's a beach ball, full of zest,
Bouncing by, it knows no rest.

So let the winds create their jest,
In shifting dunes, I feel the best.
For laughter blooms in every gust,
In this wild land, I place my trust.

Grit Beneath the Skin

Oh, grit and sand cling to my shoe,
Like tiny friends, they stick like glue.
With every step, they whisper low,
"Life's a beach, just go with the flow!"

I scrub and scrape, I laugh and sigh,
These bits of chaos, oh my, oh my!
They're like confetti from a prank,
A tiny party, gold and rank.

A grain of wisdom in my ear,
"Embrace the mess, have no fear!"
So off I go, to slide and slip,
With grit beneath my joyful trip.

In every scratch, a story's born,
Of sandy shenanigans at morn.
Who knew that poking fun could be,
A lesson wrapped in sandy glee?

Mirages of Memory

In a desert dream, I see it clear,
A soda stand that disappears!
With every sip, I taste the past,
The laughter echoes, oh so fast!

I chase the ghosts of sunny days,
Their mirthful song; a wild ballet.
A sandwich floats, a cookie drifts,
In silly shapes and quirky gifts.

But as I reach, they dance away,
Just tricks of light, a grand display.
Yet in their rise and fall, I find,
The joy of youth, forever kind.

So here's to mirages, wild and sweet,
They twirl and tease, they can't be beat.
In every blink, a giggle flows,
In the vastness, my spirit glows.

Tides of Reflection

The waves of thought come in and out,
With every splash, there's room for doubt.
In the surf, I spot my grin,
As memories and giggles spin.

I paddle out, a funny sight,
With seagulls laughing in the light.
They dive for fries, just like my mind,
In tides of jest, true joy I find.

The ocean's rhythm, a charade,
Washing worries, fun cascade.
With every roll, I shed my cares,
For laughter blooms in ocean flares.

So let the tides reflect my cheer,
As waves of humor draw me near.
In salt and sun, my spirit's free,
A splash of joy, just wait and see!

Defining the Void

In a bag of awkward moments,
I find my missing socks,
They dance with ancient wisdom,
Like penguins in flip-flops.

Empty chairs held secret chats,
While my cat plots a heist,
She steals my lunch and my heart,
A true feline living the life!

I stare at shadows on the wall,
And wonder what they think,
Do they giggle at my antics,
Or pour themselves a drink?

The vacuum hums a fable,
Of crumbs lost to the past,
As I chase my wayward dreams,
In this rollercoaster cast.

Embracing the Mirage

I chased a fleeting vision,
Of pasta dressed in gold,
Turns out it was just the sun,
And my hunger had me sold.

Mirrors reflect back my doings,
A hairdo gone askew,
I ask, 'Who's that handsome devil?',
And scream, 'It's only you!'

Dancing with a broomstick,
In a madcap living room,
I twirl and spin around it,
Like a disco ball in gloom.

My coffee spills a secret,
In a cup that's far too deep,
'Join me for a wild ride!',
Says the caffeine, not the sleep.

Beneath the Dust

Underneath my furniture,
Old memories take a nap,
They snicker at my struggles,
While plotting their comeback.

A sock puppet revolution,
Ruling from my couch abode,
With snacks for their devotion,
They launch their first episode.

Dust bunnies plot mischief,
In a kingdom filled with crumbs,
I'm their jester in the court,
Wielding laughter, not my thumbs.

So join this ragged army,
Of dust and joyful spright,
Together we'll run amok,
Spin tales both day and night.

Echoes in the Ether

I heard a joke from the breeze,
It tickled my silly face,
It whispered, 'Life's a circus,
Now go join the clownish race!'

The echoes of my laughter,
Float carried on the air,
As squirrels join the chorus,
In this nutty little fair.

An old tree groans with stories,
Of acorns lost to flight,
While branches reach like dancers,
Against the backdrop of night.

So let's toast the shenanigans,
With cups of fizzy cheer,
For echoes resonate louder,
When laughter's drawing near.

Dust and Dreams

In corners of the room, dust bunnies dance,
They twirl and spin in a crazy romance.
Whispers of dreams float on air so light,
Caught in a laugh under the moon's bright sight.

The dust of old jokes, stacked high like a mound,
Each giggle and snicker, a treasure we've found.
When swept all away, where did memories creep?
They giggle and grin, just teasing our sleep.

We build dust castles, on whim and on jest,
With rubies of laughter, we offer our best.
The dreams in the night just mill about slow,
In a whirlwind of humor and dandelion glow.

So let's raise a toast to this dust-filled delight,
Where dreams are as silly as a bird taking flight.
The world spins in laughter, let merriment flow,
In the heart of the dust, where good humor grows.

The Mirage of Identity

Who am I today? A pirate? A cat?
In a hat with a feather, I'll sit on a mat.
A cactus in cowboy boots, strumming a tune,
Under the light of a silky green moon.

My mirror is fickle, reflects what it may,
Today, I'm a spoon; tomorrow, a stray.
Perhaps I'm a sandwich, with layers so grand,
With pickles of wisdom and mustard of sand.

In the realm of absurd, I ponder and play,
Each awkward twirl is but part of the display.
A serpent? A cheeseball? The choices abound,
In this wacky parade, I'm forever unbound.

So join in the fun, take a leap, take a ride,
In the circus of life, where all quirks coincide.
No labels to wear, just a smile on my face,
In this marathon of jest, we all find our place.

Layers of Memory and Light

Beneath the old fridge, memories grow thick,
Like pickles forgotten, or that last cheese stick.
Each layer a story, stacked high in a pile,
With leftovers laughing, they cater my smile.

The light in the kitchen plays tricks on the pies,
Each slice tells a tale, amidst giggles and sighs.
Like onions on tacos, we cry with delight,
As we munch on the flavors that dance in the night.

Grandma's old recipes scribbled in haste,
With splashes and smudges, a culinary waste.
Yet there's joy in the mess, the laughter we share,
While piecing together some whimsical fare.

So gather around, with spoons made of cheer,
For the layers of laughter will echo quite clear.
In the kitchen of memory, where feasts never end,
Each bite is a giggle, each flavor a friend.

Wanderlust Within the Essence

A suitcase of giggles, I carry with pride,
Filled with dreams of the places I'll glide.
From mountains of marshmallows to lakes made of lime,
I'll travel the world one silly rhyme at a time.

The compass is broken, it spins in the air,
Pointing to nowhere, but I just don't care.
A balloon for a boat, sailing clouds up above,
With jellybean oceans, I'm lost in the love.

Each path that I wander, it tickles my nose,
As I greet every creature that plays with my toes.
A yodeling llama, or a hippo in socks,
Each friend that I meet brings more giggles than knocks.

So come take a ride on this whimsical quest,
With whimsy and laughter, we're truly blessed.
The essence of wanderlust dances around,
In the carnival of life, where pure joy is found.

The Burden of Remnants

In pockets of dust, a snack or two,
Leftovers from life, I snicker and stew.
An old sock lies here, a hat without flair,
My treasures are strange, but I don't really care.

With crumbs of my lunch still stuck in my shoe,
A smirk on my face, I can't help but chew.
Memories of yesterdays all in a pile,
I shuffle them close, selfishly smile.

In cobwebs of laughter, I trip and I fall,
Chasing my past like a moth on the wall.
Each flake tells a tale, a story absurd,
A comedy sketch, where silence is heard.

So here I stand, a hoarder of glee,
With remnants of chaos, yet wild and free.
Embracing the relics that life has bestowed,
I dance with my baggage, a light-hearted load.

Lost in the Silhouette

Wander I do, in shadows so grand,
Chasing my shape, like a silly bandstand.
A wiggle, a jiggle, I twirl in the light,
The silhouette chuckles, it gives me a fright.

From bricks of my blunders, a tower I build,
Each shape has a story, each curve is so skilled.
A bounce in my step, I move to the beat,
My shadow's my dance partner, light on my feet.

In corners of laughter, I twist and I turn,
A shadow puppet show, so vivid, I yearn.
It mimics my quirks, it follows my trails,
Through patches of sunlight and plenty of gales.

But shadows go light, in the flicker of time,
I chase my own form, a rhythm and rhyme.
With each little movement, I feel the delight,
My ghost in the sunlight, a mischievous sight.

Chronicles of Transformation

Each day is a page, a flip of the fate,
I scribble my thoughts, with laughter, I create.
From potato to dancer, my stories unfold,
I'm whirling and twirling, like marbles of gold.

In pajamas I ponder, with snacks on the side,
A taco is flung, I'll wear it with pride.
I transform my mishaps to comedy gold,
A jester at heart, with stories retold.

In mirrors I glance, a goofy old chap,
Dressed as a superhero, or maybe a sap.
Each outfit's a parable, a twist and a shout,
I'm laughing at life as I dance all about.

The chronicles shine, with laughter and cheer,
My metamorphosis brings friends near.
Each whiff of delight, each chuckle I find,
Transforms my experiences, uniquely unlined.

Drifting Particles

Floating on air, like dust in the beam,
I swirl and I twirl, like a wacky old dream.
The pollen's a party, the feathers a dance,
In the chaos of breezes, I take my chance.

Each whimsy, a thought, a giggle in flow,
In gusts and in gusties, I glide to and fro.
With fluttering laughter, I chase my own trail,
As the world spins around, I'm merrily frail.

Each fluttering bit, a confetti parade,
I drift through the moments, with little charades.
A wisp of a joke, a tickle in space,
I roll with the rhythms, no fear of the race.

Drifting, I dance, as the sunlight beams down,
Carried by whimsy, I wear fluffy gowns.
In particles of joy, I find my release,
Floating in laughter, I finally feel peace.

The Journey of Eternity

We set off on a quest, so bold,
With backpacks stuffed and tales retold.
Yet every time I check my map,
I find I'm lost, what a fine mishap!

My friend insists, 'It's right this way!'
I nod and smile, what's there to say?
We follow trails of cookie crumbs,
To find the path where laughter hums.

A mile or two, we stop for lunch,
A sandwich feast, we all will munch.
But as we eat, a dog appears,
And steals my snack, oh how it cheers!

Through twists and turns, we roam this life,
With joys and bloops, both fun and strife.
Eternity's just a twist away,
So let's get lost, and laugh all day!

A Canvas of Change

In a town where colors dance and play,
The streets reflect the hues of May.
We paint our walls with yellow dreams,
And splash on laughter, so it seems.

A painter came with brush in hand,
Said, 'Let's make beauty, oh so grand!'
But as he dipped, he lost his grip,
And sent red paint on a funny trip!

It splattered high, it splattered low,
A masterpiece of ketchup flow.
The neighbors gawked, then joined the fun,
And soon we had a paintball run!

Change is wild, it'll make you grin,
Turn your frown upside down to win.
So grab a brush, don't hesitate,
Life's a canvas—let's decorate!

From Ashes to Horizons

Once a phoenix, I thought I'd rise,
But tripped on ash—oh what a surprise!
I flapped my wings, but hit a tree,
And learned that flying's not carefree.

From flames I came, now I'm just charred,
Dazing around, the exit barred.
I laughed it off, with feathers frazzled,
Invented a dance, my joy dazzled!

My friends all came to fan the flame,
To lift my spirits, that's the game.
We roast marshmallows on my back,
And share our stories with a snack.

From ashes deep, we find our way,
Through laughter and joy, we gleefully play.
Horizons broad with joy entwined,
In every stumble, happiness we find!

Celestial Patterns in the Sand

The beach was filled with giggles and shouts,
As kids created castles, wiggled about.
Each tower built was a sight to see,
'Till one wave crashed, and they all yelled, 'Me!'

A starfish waved, thinking it was cool,
Said, 'Hey, little humans, want to rule?'
But they all just ran, oh what a sight,
Squealing and laughing, pure delight!

With every splash and grain of fun,
Our laughter echoed, under the sun.
We painted patterns with our toes,
Turned the sand into a wiggly prose.

Oh, these celestial shapes we make,
In every ripple, see how we shake!
For when life feels like slipping away,
Let's build and giggle, play all day!

Where the Wind Whispers Truths

A zephyr tickles your nose,
As it giggles and lightly flows.
Clouds toss secrets like confetti,
While grasshoppers dance, oh so petty.

The trees gossip, swaying in cheer,
Tales of squirrels and last year's beer.
The wind knows where to hide the snacks,
And hums tunes of all our quirks and lacks.

Nature's jest, on this merry ride,
With laughter echoing, we can't abide.
So listen close to what's around,
Humor hides in the softest sound.

Chasing breezy truths, we laugh,
In the cacophony of this wild gaffe.
Let's rejoice in the whispers that swirl,
For in the wind, all tales unfurl.

Soulscapes of an Eternal Voyage

In a boat made of jelly, we sail sluggishly,
Navigating dreams and thoughts wildly.
With waves that chuckle, and seagulls that grin,
Life's a riddle where silliness begins.

The stars above wink, share inside jokes,
While octopi play cards, denying blokes.
Every splash a punchline, with echoes that play,
As we drift along on this wobbly bay.

Eternal voyages in laughter we seek,
With the sun tuning in, so brightly unique.
Hiccups of joy in waves' sweet refrain,
Adventuring our hearts, a whimsical train.

So pack up your giggles, let's set sail anew,
On a sea of laughter, just me and you.
Where every turn, every wave, every swell,
Is a story worth telling, a fantastic tale.

The Currents of Human Experience

In the river of life, fish tell tales,
Of dorky ducks and their epic fails.
Turtles flip coins while crabs do the dance,
Mirth in the currents, oh what a chance!

With each ripple, a giggle may spark,
While frogs leap high, leaving us in the dark.
Every splash and a splutter, a memory made,
A rollicking journey, no plans laid.

Running with currents, we parade and frolic,
In this madcap water, joy is symbolic.
With friends who swim and bob in delight,
Ebbing and flowing through day and through night.

So paddle along, join the merriment flow,
For life's vibrant stream is a delightful show.
Each laugh is a ripple, a wave of bliss,
In the currents of living, what more could we wish?

Ephemeral Traces of Being

Footprints in pudding, oh what a sight,
A glorious mess in the morning light.
With giggles echoing and laughter abounds,
Life's precious trace in the silliest rounds.

Chasing shadows of marshmallow dreams,
Where nothing is serious as it seems.
Scavenging joy in the fluff and the fluff,
In a world that's goofy, how can we bluff?

Ephemeral giggles that dance in the breeze,
Like feathers afloat, or a sneeze that sires.
We leave our mark in this whimsical race,
Painting existence with laughter and grace.

So take a deep breath, embrace all the play,
As we sketch our stories in an odd, funny way.
These traces of being are fleeting but true,
In the joy of the moment, just me and you.

Flashes of Light

In the blink of an eye, I trip on a shoe,
Staring at stars, they wink back at you.
With a laugh and a drink, we dance in a swarm,
Mixing our stories, it's a riotous storm.

Laughter erupts, like popcorn on heat,
Jokes flying around, none missing a beat.
Fumbles and stumbles, we scatter like doves,
Chasing the giggles, oh, isn't life love?

Kites in the sky, we can hardly stay still,
Chasing the jokes, they run like a hill.
With humor like sunshine, the world feels so bright,
In flashes of fun, we find sheer delight.

Every moment is gold, just silly old chance,
Wrapped tight in the chaos, it's a whimsical dance.
Jokes hit the mark, like a dart that won't miss,
In this light-hearted game, we find endless bliss.

Fragments of a Forgotten Past

Dusty old pictures, the laughter recalls,
Like clowns at a circus, we're ready for brawls.
With hats askew, we prance through the years,
Worn-out reflections bring chuckles and cheers.

Got lost on the way, but hey, what a ride,
We'll cherish the bloopers, let humor be our guide.
Old friends from the ages, like ghosts in a play,
Jump into our jokes, let's laugh them away.

Memories flutter like birds in a suite,
With tales ever funny, they never taste sweet.
Fragments of madness, pinned up on the wall,
In each belly laugh, we're still standing tall.

The past might be hazy, but jokes are so clear,
With laughter as fuel, let's bring on the cheer.
Through winks and through giggles, we make it a blast,
Tangled in humor, we hold onto the past.

Textures of Existence

Life's like a quilt, with patterns so wild,
Each patch tells a story, like the laugh of a child.
Threads of absurdity stitch up the whole,
In textures of giggles, we sport a grand soul.

Twists and turns make for a rollercoaster ride,
Handfuls of humor we take in our stride.
The chaos is comfy, like socks that don't fit,
In strange configurations, we find our true wit.

Tickles and nudges, life's fabric is soft,
With memories woven, they never go off.
Every silly moment adds essence and flair,
In the quilt of our being, jokes dance everywhere.

Throw in a pun, mix the old with the new,
Textures of laughter adorning our view.
Start stitching your tales with biggest delight,
In the fabric of humor, everything's bright.

Shadows of What Was

Behind every corner, a shadow might laugh,
Recalling a time when we had to take half.
Witty reflections dance wide in the night,
Making mischief like we're shadows of light.

Each echo is loud, with a chuckle inside,
While prancing around, we just take it in stride.
Like ghosts at a party, we're stuck in a spin,
Spinning old tales, where the fun wouldn't thin.

What once was a blunder is now a pure jest,
Tales of our folly ignite like a fest.
Shadows grow longer, but laughter stays bright,
We sway through the past, in pure sheer delight.

So lift up your spirits, and toast to the past,
With shadows beside us, we'll have a blast.
In laughter we find what was lost in the haze,
Just riding the shadows of our funny days.